THE BUMPER BOOK OF CHAT-UP LINES

STEWART FERRIS

SUMMERSDALE

Summersdale Publishers Ltd
46 West Street
Chichester
PO19 1RP
UK

www.summersdale.com

ISBN 1 84024 126 8

Printed and bound in Great Britain by Cox & Wyman.

Thanks to Emma Burgess for her fine contributions.

What winks and is great in bed?

I don't know.

(Wink)

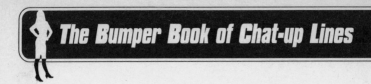

If the world was an apple, you'd be the juicy pip, and I'd like to suck it.

The world isn't an apple. It's a planet, and planets don't have pips.

What would you say is the best thing about being so gorgeous?

Not being expected to talk to ugly people like you.

What's the best way to get into your affections?

Via the North Pole.

People tell me I've got a one track mind, but the track is heading straight for you, babe. Shall we pull into the sidings and couple?

No thanks. I don't want to spoil a pleasant day by talking to you.

It must be my birthday because the sight of you is the most important gift I've ever had.

What about your natural gift for repulsing women?

I can read you like a book. I bet you're great between the covers.

I'm not letting you anywhere near my spine.

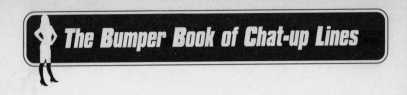

I'd like to father your children.

Fine, they're over there.

Would you like me to lick
champagne out of your navel?

There isn't any in it.

You've turned my floppy disk
into a hard drive.

*Sorry, I don't date men
with tiny peripherals.*

What time would you like me to set
the alarm for in the morning?

I don't care.
My boyfriend always gets me up.

I'd like to make love to you.

I'd rather we skipped straight
to the post-coital fag.

Would you like me to
get into your knickers?

There's already one arsehole in there,
and that's plenty.

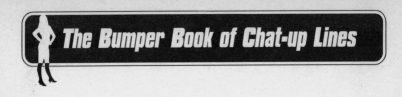

Where have you been all my life?

What do you mean – I wasn't even born for the first half of it.

Would you like a f**k . . .

No.

. . . ing drink?

Do you want to come back to my place for a pizza and a shag?

No thanks, I don't like pizza.

Do you sleep on your stomach?

No.

Can I, then?

Bond. James Bond.

Off. Piss off.

It's getting late. Why don't
we have a shag?

No thanks, I'm too tired.

Well why don't you lie down
while I have one?

The doctor said I should release
my fluids regularly. Would you mind
if I used your body as a receptacle?

I'll lend you a cup.

Hey, don't go yet . . .
you've forgotten something.

What?

Me.

Excuse me, I'm new around here. Can you give me directions to your bedroom?

I'm not very good with directions. You'd better ask my boyfriend.

Wow.

Yuk.

Would you like to come back to my place for a bacardi and grope?

Just a gin and platonic, please.

Can you tell me the time, because I want to make a note of the moment we first met?

I'll give it to you twice, because it's also the moment we split up.

Excuse me, aren't we related?

No, and I don't want to be.

Underneath these clothes I'm completely naked.

Prove it . . . to someone else.

I know a great way to burn off the calories
in that sandwich you've just eaten.

*Yes, me too, and it involves
running away from you.*

You look like you've never
done it in a water bed.

You look like you've never done it.

Can I phone you for a date?
What's your number?

It's in the phone book.

But you haven't told me your name.

That's in the phone book, too.

You remind me of the last
person I went out with.

That must be going back a bit.

Can I count on your vote?

I doubt if you can even count.

(Call her over using your finger)
I made you come using just one finger. Imagine what I could do with my whole hand!

Can you make yourself come with just one finger?

Take that jacket off and let me look at your spine.

Come any closer and I'll throw the book at you.

When I was a prisoner of war they tortured me on the rack, and it wasn't just my legs they stretched . . .

What else, then – your imagination?

Have you ever experienced puppy love?

*No, only pigeon-holing and
monkey-spanking.*

The best thing about you
would have to be my arms.

*Thanks – I would offer to shag your
brains out, but it looks as if someone
has beaten me to it.*

This is an amazing coincidence . . .
I'm single on the day that we
meet for the first time.

You'll still be single if we ever meet again.

Excuse me, I want to be served
by the most attractive waitress.
You do work here, don't you?

No, I just serve pizzas for fun.

Do you know the difference
between fellatio and focusing?

No.

Would you mind helping me adjust
my telephoto lens, then?

Are you free tomorrow night?

No, but I'm on special offer the day after.

Will you call me pretty soon?

I doubt it – you're not pretty now and I'd be surprised if that ever changed.

I'd go through anything for you.

Great, the exit's just over there.

If I could see you naked, I'd die happy.

If I could see you naked, I'd die.

Can I spend the evening with you?

I gave up baby-sitting years ago.

Can I buy you a drink?

I'd rather just have the cash.

What's a girl like you doing
in a nice place like this?

Trying to avoid you.

Save me – I'm drowning
in a sea of love!

Tough, I can't swim.

God must have cried when
you left heaven.

*Yes, and he held a huge party
when you left.*

You and me would look sweet
together on a wedding cake.

Only once you'd been cut in half.

When I look at you,
I know I've caught the love bug.

It's a pity you weren't inoculated.

I'd like to run my fingers
through your hair.

*Yes please – you can wipe
the lice on my sleeve.*

Seeing you makes my heart beat
uncontrollably fast.

The sight of you gives me heart burn.

If you were a building you
would be Versailles Palace.

And you'd be a shed.

Do you believe in magic?

*I used to, until I realised I can't
make you disappear.*

Do you believe in love at first sight?

No.

We could make beautiful music together.

I'll just fetch my earplugs, actually.

I have designs on you.

*I think you'd better go back
to the drawing board.*

Can I bury my head in your cleavage?

Just bury your head.

You're the one I've been
waiting for all my life.

Let's hope you die young.

You bring me out in a hot sweat.

You bring me out in an allergic rash.

I could get lost in your eyes.

*That's conjunctivitis,
it makes them a little foggy.*

Will you come out with me?

*Out of the closet, certainly, because meeting
you has helped me confirm my sexuality.*

I want to be really dirty with you.

You smell as if you already are.

Am I the light of your life?

No, you're far too dim.

You make my heart skip a beat.

*Only one? I was banking on
a cardiac arrest.*

I want to f**k you over and over again.

*I want to f**k you over.*

When should I phone you?

Whenever I'm not there.

I'm like quick-drying cement: after I've been laid it doesn't take me long to get hard.

I'd rather go to bed with a packet of cement.

With me you need never
fake an orgasm again.

*With you I'd rather just fake
the whole thing.*

I don't expect to have sex with you on our
first date. I'm quite restrained.

*Well I'm even more restrained. I don't even
expect to have a first date with you.*

If you go out with me I'll treat you even
better than my sports car.

*What, a good servicing every ten thousand
miles or every ten months, whichever comes
first?*

Sorry if I'm dribbling, but I had
to get drunk before I could
come and talk to you.

*It's funny how pigs don't turn into men
when they drink.*

Where do you come from?

Way above your league.

Why don't we have a holiday romance?

*Most men like you remind me
of holidays . . . they never seem
to be long enough.*

Are you as hot as me?

*I'm fine actually, but perhaps you
should get some air to your brain
by undoing your flies?*

Shall we go to your place or mine?

Both. You go to yours and I'll go to mine.

Let's be honest with each other . . . we've both come here for the same reasons.

Yes, you're right. Let's go and pull some girls.

You're most beautiful looking person I've ever seen.

So what makes you think I would want to talk to you, then?

When I'm with you I feel like a real man.

So do I.

Would you go crazy if I went out with you for a couple of months and then left you?

I'd go crazy if you went out with me for a couple of months and didn't *leave.*

If we went on a date, how would you describe me to your friends?

If I was desperate enough to date you, I wouldn't have any friends.

The Bumper Book of Chat-up Lines

You'd probably regret it in the morning if we slept together, I suppose. So how about we sleep together in the afternoon?

Your approach wasn't bad, but I'd rather see your departure.

Excuse me, were you looking at me just then?

Yes, I thought from a distance you were good looking. Sorry, I forgot my glasses.

Can I be your love slave?

Well I certainly wouldn't pay you.

You've got such a heavenly body that I've named a star after you.

By the look of your body I wouldn't be surprised if someone had named a bouncy castle after you.

Look, I won't beat about your bush, I just want to get something fairly big between us.

How about the Atlantic Ocean?

Would you like to go to bed with me tonight?

I can't – I haven't anything to wear.

I've always been fascinated by beautiful women. Mind if I study you?

Let's make it a joint project: I've always been fascinated by ugly men.

Hi, look, I'm not going to be able to date you tomorrow night, so why don't we squeeze one in tonight instead?

By the looks of you I doubt that it would be much of a squeeze.

I'm sure I've noticed you before.

I'm not sure I've even noticed you yet.

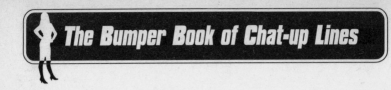

I can fulfil your sexual fantasy.

Where's your horse, then?

Excuse me, would you help me
with an itch that I can't reach?

*Sure, just rub it against the
lock on my chastity belt.*

Can you help me? I had sex
with someone last night, and I
think it might have been you.

No, I think it was with yourself.

Hello, you don't know me, but I've just come
back from the future in which you and me
have the most passionate love affair. And it
started tonight, actually.

*And I've just come back from even further in
the future where I found out that we're
brother and sister, so let's change history,
shall we?*

You know, being a millionaire
can be pretty lonely without someone
to share it with.

I'll share your money with you, if you like.

I feel like I already know you because I've
undressed you completely in my mind. Nice
body – I'd like to see more.

I did the same, but I wasn't impressed.

Would you like to wear real animal fur?

*I would if it provided an extra layer between
me and you.*

Hi, I'm from Wonderbra. We're conducting free spot checks to make sure our customers are wearing the correct size bras. Just breathe out slowly once my hands are in place . . .

When you've done I'd better check your underpants. You look as if you could benefit from a smaller pair.

Would you like to come to a
concert with me?

I've got the CD.

I'm trying to break the world kissing record
for snogging the most beautiful women in
one evening. Can I kiss you?

*Yes, but only because I'm trying to snog as
many ugly men as possible tonight, and you
would be worth double points.*

You've got great boobs.

So have you.

You look good enough to eat.

What a shame you need to diet, then.

If love is a drug, I'm addicted to you.

I recommend cold turkey.

What's your birthstone?

Breezeblock.

My body's like a temple.

*I'd have said it was more
like an amusement park.*

I could really turn you on.

*It's no big deal. I can do it myself
just by not thinking about you.*

Would you like to come for a
meal with me next week?

I've eaten.

Mind if I take your picture?

Where to?

Can I take you on a shopping trip?

Wouldn't you rather just take me in bed?

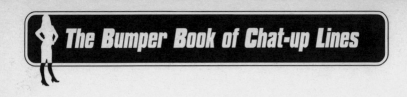

Would you like to come to bed with me?
I've got an electric blanket.

Why don't you come home with me instead?
I've got an electric chair.

Would you like to watch a sunset with me?

I've already seen one.

I would like to taste the salt
of the ocean on your lips.

Why don't you just eat a winkle?

Would you like to come to a nudist
camp with me – I could show you
what I've got to offer?

*I could see that sort of thing
in a packet of shrimps.*

Can I wash your car for you?

I don't think your hose would reach.

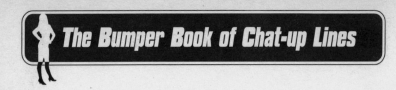

Can I fill you up, madam?

Unleaded, please.

Can I tickle your tonsils?

*I think the surgeon has
chucked them out.*

Let me have a quick stroke.

Sure, shall I call the ambulance?

I'd like to have your children.

Go ahead and take them.

People think I'm a policeman because of the size of my love truncheon.

Yes, I remember 'Inch High Private Eye'.

My yacht is stranded here for a few days until the weather improves. Want to keep me company on it?

That depends on the size of your tender.

Will you hold my beer while
I go to the toilet?

Not while it's coming out, thank you.

I don't think I've seen you
for about ten years.

*Well make the most of it, because
with a bit of luck I won't see you
for another ten.*

Will you help me choose some garden
furniture at the weekend?

I've already chosen some.

I'd like to jump into a bed with you.

OK, what about that flower bed?

Do you want to go clubbing with me?

Great, where can we find some seals?

You take my breath away.

I try, but you keep on breathing again.

Can I look up your skirt?

*Certainly. Here's the catalogue.
It's on page 57.*

Would you like to come for a drink
with me next week?

I'm not thirsty.

Can I pinch your bum?

Can I pinch your wallet?

You're irresistible.

You're resistible.

Would you like to come to a hilltop
with me next week to watch the
return of a comet that hasn't been
visible for the last thousand years?

I've seen it.

Didn't we meet in a past life?

Yes, and I wouldn't shag you then, either.

Are you a policeman, or am I wrong in
thinking that's a truncheon?

*Both . . . I am a policeman, and
it's not a truncheon.*

How would you like my
eggs in the morning?

Fertilised, please.

What's it like being the most
attractive person here?

You'll never know.

The more I drink, the prettier you get.

*There isn't enough alcohol on the planet to
make me find you attractive.*

I think we should leave together for
the sake of the other women
. . . you're making them look ugly.

*Good idea. You're making
the men look too good.*

There's something on your face,
I think it's beauty. Let me try and get it off
. . . oh, it's not coming off.

*Beauty shares the same characteristics
as my bra. It's not coming off.*

You make me melt like ice cream, you make
me boil like a kettle, and you make me
gurgle like the morning after a curry.

You need medical attention.

Let me put some fizz into your life.

OK, start by fixing my Sodastream.

I may be a bit of an eyesore, but
beauty is only a light switch away.

*You owe me a drink: you're so ugly I
dropped my glass when I saw you.*

Wasn't that you on the cover of Cosmo?

*Yes, but I've finished sitting on it now.
Want to borrow it?*

I like to think it's my vocation to make
women happy in bed.

*Let me guess: you deliver meals
on wheels to the bed-bound?*

I'd like to demonstrate to you the
sexual equivalent of a marathon.

Go ahead. I'll just watch from over there.

You make me drunk with passion, intoxicated
with love, and inebriated with desire.

*Are you absolutely sure it's got
nothing to do with the ten pints
you've drunk tonight?*

Can I see your tits?

No, they've just migrated.

Do you want to play my organ?

Only if it's got some good rhythms.

I'd like to watch you take your clothes off.

Off what?

Would you like to come for a
meal with me?

No thanks, I'm anorexic.

Fancy a champagne breakfast?

*Yes please. Get it delivered
to me tomorrow.*

Fancy a takeaway?

I wish someone would take you away.

Has anyone ever told you
how beautiful you are?

Yes, loads of people.

Why not be original and say yes?

No.

I've had part of my body pierced.
Would you like to know which bit?

Your brain.

I could make you the happiest
woman on earth.

Why, are you about to go into space?

I'd like to marry you.

I'd rather skip straight towards the divorce.

I'm a postman, so you can rely on me to deliver a large package.

Sorry, but I need someone who comes more than once a day.

I bet you a drink that you won't kiss me.

You win. Here's a drink.

You're cute.

My cute what?

I bet you my watch that you
won't let me grope you.

You win. Here's my watch.

Do you believe in love at first sight,
or should I walk past you again?

Get yourself some sturdy walking boots.

I bet you my car that you
won't have sex with me.

You win. Here's my car key.

Shall I open the door for you?

I'd rather you waited until we land.

I bet you my chest that you
won't take your bra off.

Sorry, I'm not playing anymore.

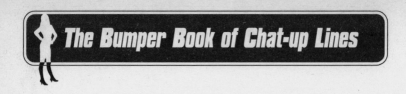
Congratulations! You've won first prize
in a competition: a date with me!

Oh. What was second prize?
Two dates with you?

Would you like my seat?

*I didn't realise transplant surgery
was so advanced.*

Hey, it's you! I nearly didn't recognise you
with your clothes on. Oh, sorry, I thought
you were an ex-lover.

*And I thought you were a future
lover . . . until you opened your mouth.*

Hello, I'm your cake. Would you
like to have it or eat it?

*I'm not hungry. I think I'll just
give it to the dog.*

I'd like to share with you
my passion for squash.

I'm not thirsty.

You've lit my fuse, I'm going to
explode with passion.

*Perhaps if we put your little fuse somewhere
wet it might go out?*

I'm thinking of giving celibacy a try.

Not with me, you're not.

What radio station would you like me to switch on in the morning?

Hospital radio.

I'd like to lick your belly-button
. . . from the inside.

Sure. Just don't burst any boils while you're there.

You look like a horse, and I'm a hedge. Would you like to jump me?

I think pruning would be a better idea.

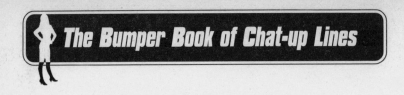

Mind if I plug my lap-top
into your modem socket?

*Isn't amazing how small they can make
them, these days?*

I'm a helicopter pilot: fancy
riding my chopper?

I'd rather just shag you.

Ever wanted to de-flower a virgin?

Nope.

It's not how big it is, it's what
you can do with it that counts.

*Well, you can certainly do something
amazing: you can make it almost
invisible to the naked eye.*

If you kiss me I promise not
to turn into a frog.

Why would I want to kiss you, then?

When I was a prisoner of war,
held captive in a tower, the other
men used part of me to climb down
the wall and escape.

Oh no, not you again?

I think it's time we introduced ourselves.

I already know myself.

I'm learning to be an artist and
I'd like to paint you.

Sure, what colour?

If I kissed you I'd go weak at the knees.

*That's probably because I'd have just given
you a good kicking.*

You're very attractive even though
if you were any more vacuous
your head would implode.

*If you were a little bit more
intelligent you'd still be stupid.*

If I told you I was well endowed
in the undercarriage department,
would you shag me?

No.

Good, because I'm
actually very small.

Are you from Jamaica?
Because Jamaican me crazy about you.

No, I'm from St Lucia.

Am I lost? I thought paradise
was further south.

*Yes, you should have turned left at the
roundabout, then take the second right. You
can't miss it.*

If you were food, you'd be caviar. If you
were a word you'd be serendipity. If you
were a car you'd be a Rolls Royce.

*If you were a real man I might stay and talk
to you.*

Are you cold, or are you smuggling
tic-tacs inside your bra?

*Are you cold or are you smuggling a
tic-tac inside your underpants?*

Women say I have the gift of the gab.

Wrap it up, then.

You remind me of a squirrel. I'd like to pile my nuts up against you.

You remind me of a rat, and I've already called the Pest Control department.

Would you like to see something swell?

Yes, the bruise I'm about to inflict on your face.

I think the sun shines out of your arse.

*Well, you're living proof that
even a turd can be polished.*

Would you mind if I take your temperature
using my special thermometer?

I always bite thermometers.

I love you.

I love chocolate, but I wouldn't bother chatting it up.

What would you say to a little f**k?

*Leave me alone, little f**k.*

Nice legs. When do they open?

Nice mouth. When does it shut?

Would you like to join me?

Why, are you falling apart?

Would you like to come
and meet my family?

OK, when are the opening hours?

Is that a gun in your pocket or
are you just pleased to see me?

No, it's a gun.

I'd like to take you out to eat.

Why won't you eat me indoors?

What would it take to get
a little kiss from you?

Chloroform.

Hello, I'm a stamp collector.

Well you're not mounting me.

Do you have a favourite singer?

*Yes, the one with two
bobbins and a foot pedal.*

There's a woman like you in
my dreams every night.

I hope she can swim.

My friends told me all about you.

What friends?

Hi there. I'd like to ask you what's
your idea of a perfect evening?

The one I was having before you came over.

I'm a musician. I'm famous for what
I can do with my little piccolo.

*That's nice. Did you say you
were a musician as well?*

I'm a meteorologist, and I'd like to study
your warm front. Let's go to an isobar and
have a drink.

*No thanks — I've seen the forecast. Damp in
parts, hot and sticky with rising cumulo
nimbus. I think I'll stay at home.*

My ideal woman has to have a
great sense of humour.

That will have to be the only sense she has.

You've got the face of an angel.

*And you've got the face of a saint
— a Saint Bernard.*

You're the best looking bloke I've ever seen.

Thanks, I wish I could say the same for you.

You could if you were as big a liar as me.

Am I the first person who has
ever tried to seduce you?

You could be — your face looks familiar.

Which part of my bed would
you like to sleep on?

The top bunk.

I've just been to the doctor. I thought I had
acute angina, but he said I was imagining it.

No, no, he's wrong — it's gorgeous.

The Bumper Book of Chat-up Lines

What would you give me if
I agreed to sleep with you?

Syphilis.

I love your crazy hair — it looks like you've
got grass growing out of it.

That's odd – I planted tulips.

You look like you haven't changed
your shirt in a fortnight.

That's impossible — I've only had it a week.

I'm a magician. Would you like me to
perform a spell for you?

OK, can you make yourself disappear?

I've come from another planet to seek out
beautiful life forms.

Is that because your race is so ugly?

I want people to love me for myself,
not my money.

Isn't that narrowing your options somewhat?

Can I introduce you to my dog, Raffles?

Oh, isn't he big? Can I stroke him?

Of course. Would you like to
stroke Raffles as well?

God ordered me to come to you.

*What's He up to? That's the fifth one this
week. I've sent all the others back.*

I never forget a face.

*Neither do I, but in your case
I'll make an exception.*

Can I have a tinkle on your piano?

I'd rather you used the toilet.

Are your legs tired? You've been running
through my mind all day.

Yeh — I was looking for a brain cell.

Do you want to know why I'm feeling sad?

There's no reason, you're just sad.

I climb mountains for a hobby, but getting on top of you is probably going to be my biggest challenge to date.

That depends on the length of your rope.

If you should happen to fall in love with me, I'll be waiting for you.

If I ever get that desperate
I won't be worth waiting for.

I saw your face in the reflection of the moonlight on the lake last night.

No you didn't.

Excuse me, is your body real?

No. You have to inflate it through my mouth every ten minutes.

Try imagining you're in love with me.

My imagination doesn't stretch that far.

The name's Thomas, John Thomas.

That's OK, I'm Holly,
so I'm used to little pricks.

Would you go to bed with
a perfect stranger?

Yes — but you're not perfect.

Don't go away
— I'm just going to put the kettle on.

Are you sure it will fit you?

When can we be alone?

When we're not with each other.

Kiss me quick.

*Don't you fancy me enough
to kiss me slowly?*

It's great that we met here tonight.
Why don't we meet up again?

Because I don't want to.

Don't you think that a man's charisma is more important than the size of his penis?

But you've got hardly any charisma either.

Shall we go and see a film?

I've seen it.

Do you think you could fall for me?

Only if you pushed me.

May I introduce myself?

Certainly — try those people over there.

Am I your dream come true?

I don't know yet. Go and stand in the road with your eyes closed, and we'll see.

You must tell me your name.

*It begins with 'Mrs'.
Shall I bother to continue?*

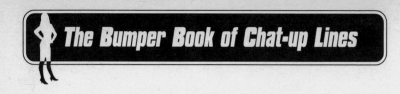

You really set me on fire.

Oh good, I didn't think I used enough petrol.

If I had known I was going to meet someone as amazingly lovely as you, I'd have had my nostrils plucked.

And if I'd known I was going to meet someone as ugly as you, I'd have had my eyeballs plucked.

Do you think it was fate that
brought us together?

No. It was just bad luck.

Would you like to come out with
me for some coq au vin?

What sort of van do you drive?

When I roll across my satin sheets at night,
the sound reminds me of you.

What, while I'm eating a packet of crisps?

When I look at the stars I see your eyes. When I look at a flower I smell your perfume. When I look at the sun I feel your warmth.

When I look at a cow I see your bullshit.

I've heard you're a good cook, but there is no recipe for my love for you.

What about Mini Sausages with Leeks?

Look, to decide whether or not we should date, let's toss for it.

No, let's just flip a coin. Heads — you don't get to go out with me, tails — I don't get to go out with you. Fair?

What would you say is my best feature?

Your ornamental pond.

I'm considering chucking my girlfriend for you. How do you feel about that?

But I don't want your girlfriend.

Don't go — you'll never find anyone like me again.

I certainly hope not.

Where can I find mutual love?

At the beginning of a tennis match.

My stars said I would meet the
woman of my dreams tonight.

I'll go and see if I can find her for you.

Where can we go from here?

I don't care, so long as you go first.

Can I have your name?

Why — haven't you already got one?

It's OK, we can be together tonight. I've given my girlfriend the evening off.

What for, good behaviour?

I've always believed in love at first sight.

So did I — until I met you.

I've lost my script, so we'll have to ad-lib.

I don't think much of your part, anyway.

Can I kiss you?

*Of course, but mind you don't
burn yourself on my cigarette.*

Do you mind if I smoke?

I don't care if you burn.

I'm sure I could turn you on.

You couldn't even turn on a radio.

Hello. Didn't we sleep together once?
Or was it twice?

It must have been once.
I never make the same mistake twice.

You seem to me like a sensible girl.

That's right — I won't go
anywhere near you.

You would be great to go on a camping holiday with. Separate tents, of course.

I'd prefer separate campsites.

Would you like a nibble of my sausage?

Not yet. Let's eat first.

Do I get the impression that you're playing hard to get?

No, I'm playing impossible to get.

I've got some condoms, so I think
we should sleep together right now.

*What's the hurry? Are they close
to their expiry date?*

Do you come here often?

Not if you do.

You're very pretty, but your eyes indicate
you've had a sheltered life.

They've only been sheltering from you.

Do you kiss with your eyes closed?

I would if I were kissing you.

Hey, you're not much of a looker,
but I'll have you.

Thanks. You must be very open-minded.
Was that how your brain slipped out?

Oi, darling, do you want to really enjoy
yourself with me?

Sorry, I couldn't possibly entertain
the thought of spending time with
someone who splits infinitives.

No, I'll pay for you as well.

You're utterly beautiful, but there must be something about you that's less than perfect: I expect you're a hopeless cook.

True, so I suppose Nature's compensated you with perfect cooking abilities, then?

Shall we go all the way?

Yes, as long as it's in different directions.

Would you accept if I were to ask you out?

Accept what — defeat?

You don't sweat much for a fat lass.

I will when I start running away from you.

I had no idea I would ever
meet someone like you in here.

*I had no idea they would ever
let someone like you in here.*

I'd like to see more of you.

There isn't any more of me.

I think I could make you very happy.

Why, are you leaving?

It's funny, I know I'm a bit drunk, well, very drunk, but I'm sure I know you from somewhere. Any chance of a kiss?

Hello Dad.

Hi. I'm a tenor.

Sorry, I've only got a fiver.

Go on, don't be shy: ask me out.

OK, get out.

What happened to your face? Do you step on rakes for a hobby?

No, I impersonate you.

Didn't we used to be lovers?

*Yes. I left you because you have an
infuriating memory problem.*

I don't remember that.

You have a peach-like complexion
— pale and wrinkly.

*You don't look like a peach,
but your breath smells as if you've been
eating them. A week ago.*

Your face is familiar
— I might even say commonplace.

*Yours must have been limited edition —
limited because no one else
wanted one like it.*

Your face is absolutely perfect.

So is yours . . . for radio.

You're the kind of girl I'd like to take home
to mother except I can't trust my father.

*Don't worry — he's not the sort to drink
from the same cup twice.*

You've got everything a man could want:
teeth, hair, moustache . . .

All I lack is your charm and subtlety.

Will you come out with me on Saturday?

*Sorry, I'm having a
headache at the weekend.*

Can I have your phone number?

No, but you can have my dialling code.

Would you mind if I take a lock of your hair?

Why, are you trying to stuff a mattress?

Where did you get those big blue eyes?

They came with my face.

You're just my type — you're a girl.

I'm just my type as well, I'm afraid.

You look like my fourth wife.

How many have you had?

Three.

Did you know that men with the biggest dicks have the smallest mouths?

I could park my car in your mouth.

I'm not interested in a relationship, but I don't feel like being alone tonight.

Are you asking for a shag, or what?

You must be a Mars bar, because I'm a chocoholic and I want you badly.

You're certainly doing badly.

I haven't done this sort of thing before. I want you to teach me.

OK, you go out of that door, close it gently behind you, and go away.

Shall we go somewhere quieter?

No need — I've got some earmuffs you can borrow.

I'd go to the ends of the world for you.

Yes, but would you stay there?

Please talk to me so that creep
over there will leave me alone.

I just said that to someone about you.

Shall I tell you my name?

Why?

So you'll know what to scream.

May I have a drag on your fag?

That's ironic — actually I am a fag in drag.

Let's skip the awkward beginning and pretend that we have known each other for a while. So, how's your Mum?

She told me I wasn't to see you any more.

You look like a model.

No, I'm real.

You've got a smile that could light up a whole town.

You've got a mouth that could accommodate a whole town.

You're so hot you melt the
elastic in my underwear.

I wondered what the smell was.

What would you say if I
asked you to marry me?

*Nothing. I can't talk and laugh
at the same time.*

Listen, I want to tell you something
. . . I'm not wearing any underwear.

*Don't worry — there's a shop just round the
corner where you can get some.*

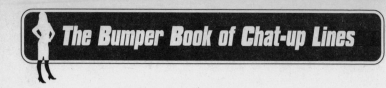

What sign were you born under?

'No entry'.

I miss my teddy bear.
Will you sleep with me?

Here, borrow mine.

Is it hot in here or is it just you?

It's hot.

Is your daddy a thief?

No.

Then how did he steal the stars out of the
sky and put them in your eyes?

Is your daddy a thief?

Yes.

Can he get me a cheap video?

I like every muscle in my body.
Especially yours.

*What's a girl like you doing in a
nice place like this?*

Hey, don't I know you?

Not yet. Ask me another.

Before I buy you a drink,
can you tell me if you like me?

*Get the drink first.
We'll deal with the bad news later.*

Do you know what would
look good on you?

No?

Me.

Going my way? Can I walk with you?

You can walk near me.

If I told you that you have a beautiful body,
would you hold it against me?

No, I'd just hit you.

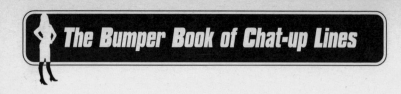

How about coming back to my
place for a bit of heavy breathing?

Why, is the lift broken?

Do you know where we are?

Why?

Because I'm lost in your eyes.

Do you have the number for heaven?

Why?

It looks like they've lost an angel.

Where shall we go for our honeymoon?

What about Finland?
And I'll go to New Zealand.

Will you join me in a glass of wine?

I don't think there'd be room for both of us.

Can I borrow ten pence?
I want to call my mother and thank her.

I'd complain if I were you.

Can I have directions?

To where?

To your heart.

Feel a muscle, any muscle.

All these curves, and me with no brakes.

Can I borrow your phone?

Why?

My ex told me to call
when I fell in love again.

Can I flirt with you?

I was hoping to meet someone a little younger. People might think you're my mother.

I'd like to take you to dinner.

Sure — can you pick me up again afterwards?

Good evening. I'm conducting research to find my ideal partner, and I'd like to ask you a couple of questions: will you come to bed with me, and if so how much do you charge?

Yes, I'll go to bed with you, and I don't normally charge, but for you I'd make an exception.

Do you get out of the bath
to go to the toilet?

No need — I bathe in the toilet.

Where is the toilet?

Oh, I didn't realise you were house trained.

You probably think I'm mad coming up to
you like this, but I have this strange urge to
buy you a drink.

*I don't want anything to do with your
strange urges.*

Weren't you at the party last week?

*Yes. And I haven't changed my
mind since then, I'm afraid.*

I'm afraid I'm an incurable romantic.

Well, you're incurable, that's for sure.

I've waited all my life to meet you.

Stuck at the back of the queue, were you?

Virtually everyone here is ugly except you.

Well you're so ugly I bet your psychiatrist makes you lie face down on the couch.

Very difficult getting served here. What are you having in case I get served first?

An attack of nausea.

Most guys are like public toilets; either vacant, engaged or full of crap.
Which are you?

Er, could you repeat the question?

Kiss me.

You'll have to drug me first.

Will you sleep with me.

No, I'm an insomniac.

What would you do if you ever got chatted-up by a woman?

Warn her that I used to be one.

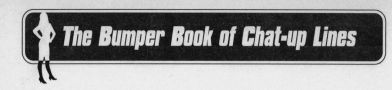

The trouble with this place is some of the people that come here.

Do something about it — leave.

Shall we introduce ourselves?

I already know myself. What about you?

You'd look good in anything but the mirror.

At least I've got a mirror.

Ring me sometime. Must dash now,
but here's my number.

Don't you have a name?

Shall we share a taxi to the nightclub?

*I wouldn't even share the earth
with you if I had a choice.*

Queuing is so boring, don't you find?

It is now.

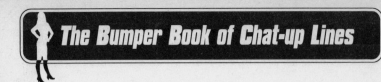

Please take a seat.

Where to?

'Yes' is my favourite word. What's yours?

No.

How did you get to be so beautiful?

I must have been given your share.

On a scale of one to ten, you have been
voted ten by everyone over there.
How do you feel?

I use my fingertips.

Can you give me your name, please?

I don't think 'Melissa' would suit you.

Nobody I know can tell me who you are, but
I'm sure I've seen you before.

*Why don't you take that ugly mask off so
that I can see what you look like?*

No, don't tell me: you're a Pisces?

OK, I won't tell you.

Very nice gear you've got on.

Yeh, and it's staying on.

Quick, the lights are coming back
on in a minute. Kiss me.

No. I'm your wife.

I love your hair.

Which one?

My friend fancies you.

You just keep your friend in his underpants, out of trouble.

May I have the pleasure of this dance?

No, I'd like some pleasure too.

I don't normally do this sort of thing, but here's my card — I'd like to meet you some time.

You just did.

Keep it up — you're doing well.

I wish I could say the same for you.

Life has been empty without you.

I'm not letting you fill me up.

Isn't it boring here?
Do you want to go somewhere else?

*You go — that will be enough
to liven things up.*

Are you sisters?

Yes.

You must have left Cinderella at home.

I'm raising money for charity by
charging for kisses.

Never mind the kisses, just take the money.

I've been given a couple of tickets for the play on Thursday — do you want to come?

Only if you give me both of them.

I don't suppose you would be interested in going out one night to see a film?

I'm already booked that night.

I'm a doctor: what's your appendix doing tonight? I'd love to take it out.

Very funny. You should be on the television then I could turn you off.

Going so soon?
Stay a minute and let me get you a drink.

Just give me the cash — I'll get one later.

Fancy a swim?

I can't swim, so shall we jump straight to the bit where you resuscitate me?

Got a light?

Yes thanks.

Um, hello.

Oscar Wilde, I presume?

Every time I come here I've seen you.
I'd like to know more about you.

So would the police.

Forgive me for being so forward,
but I think I love you.

Come back and see me when you're certain.

Don't drink the beer here.
It's awful. Try my saliva instead.

Got any nuts?

Do you like my new jacket?

It's great. Shame your body
doesn't suit it, though.

Can I buy you a drink?

*I would think so
— why don't you ask the barman?*

Your face or mine?

His.

Excuse me: I don't normally talk to strange
women in the street, but I'm on my way to
confession and I'm a bit short of material.

Try the draper's shop.

I always swallow.

Good. You'd starve otherwise.

Let's eat out. How about Japanese?

I'm a bit short-sighted, so don't have the raw fish, or I won't know which end of you is which.

What's the biggest problem in your life?

Look in a mirror.

I've forgotten your name but I'll never forget your face. I'm reminded of it every morning when I hop on the back of the bus.

Why would you hop on a bus? Wouldn't it be easier to use both legs?

Have you ever tried drinking Australian wine?

What else would I be doing with it?

I've seen your beautiful face before, I'm sure.

Yes, I'm a friend of your wife's.

I'm fat, I'm ugly, I'm hairy, I'm smelly, and I fart like a wind tunnel. But I'm bloody rich.

I don't want you thinking I'm just after your money, darling. What's your name?

You show me yours, I'll show you mine.

OK, my boyfriend's over there.

Do you take the washing-up out of the sink before you piss into it?

No. Nor after.

Hi. I'm on a computer date, actually, but the computer hasn't shown up. Do you want to join me instead?

No, I never date men with tiny peripherals.

Er, hello. My name's, er
. . . I can't remember.

That's a lovely name.

I like the way you dye your roots brown.

At least I've got roots.

What do you think of the music here?

Better than the company.

Umpteen people must have already told you this, but you're very beautiful.

You're so ugly, Frankenstein's Monster would go to a Halloween party as you.

You know what I like most about you?
All of you.

That's great, because I'm an all or nothing sort of person, and with you it's nothing.

I'd like to cook for you — I'm a great cook.

No thanks, I'm not much of an eater.

Hello.

Goodbye.

Have you got a problem with that?

No, only with you.

Have you got any Irish in you?

No.

Would you like some?

Yes please. Mine's a Guinness.

Cheer up darling, it may never happen.

It just has.

Can you see me in your future?

No. You're already in my past.

With you I've finally found what I've been looking for in life.

With you I've finally lost it.

Kiss me and I'll tell you a secret.

I know your secret - I work at the clinic.

How do you keep an idiot in suspense?

Don't know.

Nor me. Been waiting for someone to tell me, actually.

I've got a condom with your name on it.

You must be mistaken.
My name's not Durex Extra Small.

Would you like another drink?

Do you really think our relationship
will last that long?

Have you ever done it with a real man?

No, why - have you?

Are you happy?

I was.

If I could dance, I'd ask you to dance, but I can't. If I could sail, I'd take you sailing, but I can't. However, I'm the father of twelve kids. How about it?

Would you like my ship
to sail into your port?

No. It's an airport.

Haven't I seen your face before
— on a police poster?

*Look who's talking — I bet when you go to
the zoo you have to buy two tickets: one to
get in and another to get out.*

When will we meet again?

In another life, I hope.

Are you separated?

No, it's just the way I walk.

Do you know what I am?

A eunuch?

Are you a miner?

No.

Oh, so that's not a pickaxe in your pocket?

How would you like your
eggs in the morning?

Unfertilised, mate. Piss off.

What's your favourite record?

Sebastion Coe's 1500 metres.

What's your favourite film?

Kodak.

You have the bluest eyes I've ever seen.

Thanks. I only had them resprayed yesterday.

I'm a photographer for a model agency:
I've been looking for a face like yours.

I'm a plastic surgeon.
I've been looking for a face like yours.

I drive a Formula One racing car.

So why were you late?

I work in the music business.

I know, I've been to your shop.

I've circumnavigated the
world single-handed.

*What were you doing with
your other hand, then?*

What's your favourite flower?

Self-raising.

How can I prove my love for you?

In a court of law.

Do you believe in sex before marriage?

*In general, yes, but with
you I'd make an exception.*

Do you fancy coming for a
walk in the woods?

What for — to meet your family?

I want people to like me for what I am.

Is that why you drive a Porsche?

What's your favourite French dish?

Eric Cantona.

Have you had a wonderful evening?

Sure, but it wasn't this one.

**More humour books
are available via our website
(including *How To Chat-up Men* and
How To Chat-up Women)**